SUGGESTIONS FOR GR

1 THE ROOM	Discourage people from sitting ⌐ ‾‾‾‾ - all need to be equally involved
2. HOSPITALITY	Tea or coffee on arrival can b⌐ Perhaps at the end too, to encou⌐ Some groups might be more ambi⌐ ....ars to bring a dessert to start the evening (even in Lent, hospitality is OK!) with coffee at the end.
3. THE START	If group members do not know each other well, some kind of 'icebreaker' might be helpful. You might invite people to share something quite secular (where they grew up, holidays, hobbies, significant object, etc.) or something more 'spiritual' (one thing I like and one thing I dislike about my church/denomination). Place a time limit on this exercise.
4. PREPARING THE GROUP	Take the group into your confidence, e.g. 'I've never done this before', or 'I've led lots of groups and each one has contained surprises'. Sharing vulnerability is designed to encourage all members to see the success of the group as their responsibility. Encourage those who know that they talk easily to ration their contributions. You might introduce a fun element by producing a bell which all must obey instantly. Encourage the reticent to speak at least once or twice – however briefly. Explain that there are no 'right' answers and that among friends it is fine to say things that you are not sure about – to express half-formed ideas. But, of course, if individuals choose to say nothing, that is all right too.
5. THE MATERIAL	Encourage members to read next week's chapter before the meeting. It helps enormously if each group member has their own personal copy of this booklet – hence the reduced rate when 5 or more copies are ordered. There is no need to consider all the questions. A lively exchange of views is what matters, so be selective. If you wish to spread a session over two or more meetings, that's fine. You might decide to replay all or part of the audio tape/CD – the closing reflection for example – at the end. For some questions you might start with a few minutes' silence to make jottings. Or you might ask members to talk in sub-groups of two or three, before sharing with the whole group.
6. PREPARATION	Decide beforehand whether to distribute (or ask people to bring) paper, pencils, hymn books, etc. If possible, ask people in advance to read a Bible passage or lead in prayer, so that they can prepare.
7. TIMING	Try to start on time and make sure you stick fairly closely to your stated finishing time.

TRANSCRIPT

A word-by-word TRANSCRIPT of the audio tape/CD is available. GROUP LEADERS in particular may find this helpful in their preparation, whilst other group members may wish to have a transcript for easy reference. (See centre pages of this booklet.)

SESSION 1

... when we SEEK HAPPINESS?

'God is not interested in your *happiness*; he is very interested in your *holiness*'. I clearly remember that confident declaration from a sermon I heard over thirty years ago. It is certainly memorable, but is it true?

In the middle of the twentieth century, J B Phillips produced a justly famous paraphrase of the New Testament. When he came to the Beatitudes (Matthew 5.1-12) he did not employ the customary 'Blessed are ...' Instead, he used the word 'happy'.

- How *happy* are the humble-minded, for the Kingdom of Heaven is theirs!
- *Happy* are those who claim nothing, for the whole earth will belong to them!
- *Happy* are those who are hungry and thirsty for goodness, for they will be truly satisfied!

If J B Phillips is right, Jesus is very concerned for our happiness. But as the teacher from Nazareth insists that happiness is a by-product of holiness, perhaps that preacher wasn't wrong after all.

In the upside-down world of the Gospels, Jesus sets out his recipe for happiness. True happiness comes from poverty of spirit, mourning and persecution, among other things. Oceans of ink have been spilt in trying to work out exactly what Jesus meant by that remarkable sequence of memorable paradoxes. But the main point is clear enough. Make happiness your aim and you will miss the target. Feed your desire for happiness with a diet of possessions and popularity, or a ruthless search for excitement and success, and you will shoot very wide indeed.

Here, as always, the first will be last and the last will be first. If you want to find true happiness there is only one way. You must 'lose yourself' (Mark 8.35) by focusing on the needs of others, not on your own wants.

Martyrs or 'Martyrs'?

Most of us are very clever at disguising our true intentions and hiding our real objectives, even from ourselves. We've all met people with a martyr complex – those who draw attention to themselves and feed their egos by making a display of their insignificance or hard work for others.

Getting the balance right is never easy, and in an attempt to correct the 'I am a worm' approach to holiness, many modern Christian writers encourage

> I do approve of religion. I think everybody should try church before they try therapy. It's extremely healthy for you to spend an hour a week thinking not about what a victim you are, but how wicked you are.
>
> *Fay Weldon*

> The Christian emphasis is not on self-fulfilment and self-preservation, but on a giving-away of the self in relationship to others and the Other.
>
> *Paul Goodliff*

> If you're downcast and gloomy, the fresh wind of God's Spirit can, and often does, give you a new perspective on everything and, above all, a sense of God's presence, love, comfort, and even joy. But the point of the Spirit is to enable those who follow Jesus to take into all the world the news that he is Lord.
>
> *Bishop Tom Wright*

> God is not constrained to create – there is nothing he needs from creation that he does not already possess ... God creates out of nothing, and simply for joy, for fun, you might say.
>
> *Jane Williams*

us to love ourselves. They insist that 'loving our neighbour as ourselves' involves just that – loving ourselves. I am not convinced. I suspect that when Jesus quoted that great Old Testament maxim, he was not encouraging us to love ourselves. He knew that most of us do that quite enough already. The commandment has its focus on our *neighbour,* not ourselves.

Of course we must recognise that self-hatred and self-harm exist. And low self-esteem can be very damaging. But perhaps we need to recognise, too, that far more of us are likely to fall into the trap of self-indulgence and self-regard. Most of the time I suspect that I need to be *tougher,* not easier, on myself, whatever the pop psychologists and theologians might say.

Some readers may disagree strongly with this line of argument. That's fine. The whole purpose of this course is to generate lively discussion, deep thought and – we hope – appropriate action. If you disagree with me, convince your group that I am wrong and you are right!

Perhaps the secret is to be found in the old Greek adage: 'Know thyself'. If I know that I am one of this world's natural pleasure-seekers, then I will be on my guard against temptations which lead me to self-indulgence. If, on the other hand, I know myself to be a natural 'martyr', I will refuse to indulge this tendency. Instead, I will make time for myself and enjoy the freedom for which 'Christ has set us free' (Galatians 5.1).

Great Bible words

If some of the above sounds rather dour, what follows is much more cheerful. The word 'happiness' may not be found frequently in the Bible, but an outstanding near equivalent certainly is.

* *Joy* is one of the great words which tumble from the New Testament letters. It is found in that lovely list of qualities described by St Paul as the fruit of the Spirit (Galatians 5.22-23). Christian discipleship is not simply a matter of grim duty. There are plenty of 'oughts' in the Christian life, but in essence it is a new quality of life, produced by the Spirit of the risen Christ within us. He works in us and we work with him. This is the secret of Christian living and the long-term outcome is, or should be, a character marked by love and tranquillity – with a generous pinch of laughter too, perhaps.

- The second great Bible word which relates to happiness is *peace*. Peace of mind and inner contentment are wonderful attributes, as we know when we recognise them in others. Peace may suggest stillness and inactivity but this need not be the case. The risen Lord stood among his amazed – and terrified – disciples and uttered a memorable phrase. Those words are his glorious gift to his followers in every generation: 'Peace be with you'. It was not long before they were out in a hostile world, undertaking breath-taking feats of bravery and expending enormous energy in spreading the good news. The New Testament bears witness to the fact that they took the peace of Christ with them into every situation, however turbulent. With St Peter, they learned how to 'cast all their cares upon him, for he cares for you' (1 Peter 5.7).

*

Where is God when we seek happiness? He is at our shoulder, urging us on, longing that we should discover that the route to lasting happiness is the way of true holiness. And holiness is a cocktail of obedience, service, humility, exuberance, openness, generosity, sparkle, joy and quiet contentment.

A person is a person
only because of others
and on behalf of others.

African proverb

QUESTIONS FOR GROUPS

Please read page 1 (especially paras 4 and 5) before starting. Some groups will not have time to consider more than a few questions. That is fine; this is not an obstacle course!

SUGGESTED BIBLE READING:
Luke 6.20-26

1. Raise any points from this booklet or the audio tape/CD with which you strongly agree or disagree.

2. What makes you happy? What makes you sad? Describe the happiest time of your life.

3. Describe the happiest person, the saddest person, and the holiest person that you know or know about.

4. (a) What, in your view, are the ingredients of a truly happy life? Have your views on this changed over the years? If so, how?

   (b) How does happiness relate to holiness?

5. Re-read the final paragraph. Does this relate to your experience of life and your understanding of holiness?

6. Is your church a place of contagious joy and happiness? Mark it on a scale of 1 to 5 (1=poor; 5=miraculous!). How could you improve your score?

7. How does happiness relate to joy, pleasure, peace of mind and possessions?

8. How does happiness relate to health, people, prayer and worship?

9. **Read the Beatitudes (Matthew 5.1-12).** What on earth does Jesus mean by verses 3, 4, 5 and 11?

10. **Read Mark 8.34-37** and **12.29-31**.

    (a) What does Jesus mean by his paradox about losing life in order to find life?

    (b) Does it work in practice?

    (c) Is there a place for assertiveness in the Christian life?

Closing meditation:

'The joy of the LORD is your strength'
    (Nehemiah 8.10)

Re-read the Boxes. Then, in silence, give thanks for those who have inspired you and pray for anyone you know to be unhappy. Then say the Grace together.

Making full use of the CD

- To make the CD which accompanies this course even easier to use, we have incorporated multiple indexing tabs. Should you wish to make use of them, these allow you to find the start of each new question posed to the participants by Simon Stanley, the presenter. For further convenience, the tab numbers are shown in the Transcript booklet.

- To reassure those not familiar with CD technology, these tabs are silent and do not in any way interfere with the playing of the sound track. As before, you can simply press the start button and let each session run!

SESSION 2

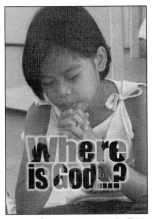

Where is God ...?

... when we FACE SUFFERING?

In AD 156, old Bishop Polycarp of Smyrna stood in a pagan stadium. He was challenged to deny Jesus Christ and embrace the pagan gods. He declared, 'I have been his servant for 86 years and he has never done me any wrong. How then can I blaspheme my king who has saved me?' He was executed by burning.

Inflicted suffering

When Singapore was captured by the Japanese during the Second World War, Leonard Wilson, an Englishman, was Bishop there. Like many others, he was tortured. When other prisoners were too ill to cope, he volunteered to take their beatings. Knowing him to be a Christian, one of his interrogators asked, 'Why doesn't your God save you?' Bishop Wilson's memorable reply was, 'He does save me – not by removing the pain but by giving me the strength to bear it.'

After the war he conducted a Confirmation Service in Singapore Cathedral. As he placed his hands on one candidate, the Bishop recognised him. The man he was confirming into the Christian faith was one of his tormentors. That man had come to faith as a result of Leonard Wilson's witness in prison.

This reminds me of the martyrdom of Stephen and the conversion of Saul, who became Paul the apostle. He was present at Stephen's stoning (Acts 7.54-60). It seems highly likely that Stephen's courage in witnessing to his faith in Jesus Christ played a crucial part in Paul's conversion.

Both incidents show that great good can come out of terrible suffering. Both incidents also show that suffering can be experienced and endured with inspiring fortitude.

Numerous other examples come to mind. Space allows for just one. In 177 AD the Christians in Lyons were subjected to cruel persecution. The early historian, Eusebius, recorded the events of those days. The believers were mocked and tortured in an arena. Blandina, a slave, wore down her tormentors with her endurance, so they put her back in prison.

Later they brought her into the arena again, where she was killed by a bull. 'And so', wrote Eusebius, 'she travelled herself along the same path of conflicts as they [her fellow Christians] did, and hastened to them, rejoicing and exulting in her departure.'

Contrast*

The peace and serenity – and sense of the *presence* of God – displayed by Blandina, is characteristic of the Christian martyrs since the death of Stephen. They

*Footnote: Material in this section is based on *Teach Yourself Christianity* (Hodder & Stoughton) also by John Young.

showed a deep, even joyful, sense of God's sustaining presence. *This is in sharp contrast with the death of Jesus.*

We find there a *lack* of serenity: he was 'in anguish of spirit'. We find there a *lack* of peace: 'Father, if it be your will, take this cup from me.' We find there a *lack* of a sense of the presence of God: 'My God, my God, why have you forsaken me?'

For those who died *for* Christ – a constant sense of the presence of God. For Jesus as *he* died – a sense of abandonment by God, and of utter loneliness. The New Testament faces this immense puzzle and comes up with a remarkable answer. The martyrs, in suffering for their faith, experienced physical pain. So did Jesus. But for him there was an extra – and hugely significant – factor. Jesus suffered *uniquely* and *spiritually*. On the cross, he was locked in battle with the forces of darkness. It is a battle which he won, so John the Baptist could declare that Jesus is 'the Lamb of God who takes away the sin of the world' (John 1.29).

He is also the One who comes alongside us when we suffer. I recall a conversation with a woman whose child had died. She told me that the Bible had given her great comfort. I asked if she had a particular passage in mind, expecting her to speak about eternal life or the presence of Christ. To my surprise she quoted those bleak words of Jesus from the cross, 'My God, my God, why have you forsaken me?' 'You see', she went on, 'Jesus knows just how I feel.'

Jesus' cry of dereliction was, for her, an affirmation – not a denial – of faith in God. She found solace in the remarkable fact that, on the cross, Jesus suffered *with* us as well as *for* us. He immersed himself in the bitter pains of a suffering world. In doing so, he shared our pain and brought to us the gift of redemption.

The suffering which inspires

A great deal of suffering is not inflicted by other people. It comes to us, unbidden, through illness or accident. Such suffering can embitter and diminish. Many of us can think of people who have become angry or sullen as a result of their unhappy circumstances.

But suffering seems to *soften* hearts too – perhaps more often than it hardens them. I think of a young couple whose child suffered a cot death. For years the husband had wrestled with Christianity. Perhaps surprisingly, he came through that devastating experience as a convinced believer.

I have many inspiring friends who, like that father, have suffered terribly and whose faith in Christ has been a source of strength over many years. Molly, for example, has had far more than her fair share of suffering. Happily married with two young children, her husband died suddenly and unexpectedly. She soldiered on and drew strength, companionship and love from her two daughters. One day, a policeman came with the news that her younger daughter, Sally, had been killed in a road accident. She was twenty-one.

That was over twenty years ago and throughout that time Molly has struggled with ill-health. Yet to visit her is a delight. Her gratitude towards those who care for her is moving. Her deep faith in the God who strengthens her and – because of the cross – suffers with her and understands what she is going through, is inspiring. Molly doesn't say 'Why me?' but 'Why not me?.'

So does Eileen. She is a teacher who needed to take early retirement because she suffers from multiple sclerosis. She continues to lead a full and purposeful life, although her mobility is severely limited. Among other things she is a very effective fundraiser for *Save the Children.*

Eileen has a quiet faith. She doesn't feel angry at God for 'sending MS'. She recognises that illness and accidents are facts of life. She realises that suffering is a problem which makes belief in God difficult for some people – but not for her. Eileen feels supported by friendship and by prayer. She retains her sense of humour and her peace of mind, as an extract from one of her letters makes clear. (See Box in margin.)

I've had to give up driving. The fatigue is rotten, but not such a worry now that I've stopped working. The blurred and double/triple vision is a nuisance, but curiously interesting – for example the Cathedral has had two spires for a couple of years, there are three moons in the sky and an awful lot of eight-legged cats about! I am quite used to it now and it's not a worry. I've made no retirement plans, confident that something will emerge for me, when the time is right.

A very public death

As a young man Karol Wojtyla was extremely gifted, physically, intellectually and socially. He enjoyed swimming and mountain walking; he wrote poetry and plays.

As an adult he was in the public eye as Pope John Paul II. For the last ten years of his life he suffered from Parkinson's disease, but he chose to continue his very public ministry right to the end.

A brilliant linguist and superb communicator, he may have been tempted to hide from public gaze by the time he was struggling to utter a single word. But he resisted that temptation and appeared in public as a vulnerable old man who was entirely dependent upon others. In this way he dignified suffering and death.

One of the most difficult aspects of modern life is feeling helpless as we stand by and observe the suffering of those whom we love. By choosing this path to death, Pope John Paul gave inspiration and strength to many who find themselves in this predicament. Little wonder that vast crowds gathered to celebrate his life and mourn his death.

QUESTIONS FOR GROUPS

SUGGESTED BIBLE READING:
2 Corinthians 1.1-7

1. Raise any points from this booklet or the audio tape/CD with which you strongly agree or disagree.

2. Reflect on your own suffering, or on the suffering of someone known to you – perhaps someone who, like Molly and Eileen, has triumphed over adversity. What have you learned from these experiences?

3. In your view, was Pope John Paul II right to struggle on despite Parkinson's disease? Or should he have given way to a younger, fitter man?

4. Do you know of people who have been

   (a) embittered by suffering? (b) softened by suffering?

   Why does faith so often seem strong among people who suffer famine and natural disasters?

5. Re-read the Box on page 8 about martyrs. Does this surprise you? How can you, your group or your church support fellow Christians in severe need or people undergoing torture?

6. Because Christianity is not 'trendy' or 'cool' in Britain today (unlike some other places e.g. Poland, Africa), young people sometimes suffer for their Christian witness. How would you encourage a young person who is bullied at school because of his/her faith?

7. A Sikh group visits your church and you are asked what the suffering and death of Jesus mean to you personally. How would you respond?

8. A neighbour has lost a beloved grandchild and wants to talk to you about faith, doubt, prayer and heaven. His wife wants to visit a medium but he is sceptical. Imagine this conversation. What might he say and how would you respond?

9. **Read Matthew 28.20b** and **2 Corinthians 1.3-7** and **8.9**. What significance do these famous verses have for you?

10. **Read Matthew 26.26-30.** The Eucharist, the Church's central act of worship, focuses on the suffering of Jesus. A young person asks, 'What does Holy Communion mean to you?' How would you answer?

Closing meditation:

'But my strength is made perfect in weakness'
(2 Corinthians 12.9)

Re-read some of the Boxes. In silence, pray for friends, neighbours and relatives who are suffering. Then say the Lord's Prayer together.

SESSION 3

... when we MAKE DECISIONS?

Personal decisions

Simone Weil was a brilliant Frenchwoman whose life was crammed with tough, controversial decisions. She was a philosophy teacher, but she chose to identify with ordinary people by working in France's vineyards and in the Renault car factory.

During the Second World War Simone came to England to work for the French provisional government. Throughout that period she identified with her own Nazi-dominated country as completely as possible. She refused to eat more food than she would have received in occupied France. As a result she became ill. Simone died penniless in 1943 and was buried in a 'pauper's grave'.

It is clear that Simone Weil faced a whole series of difficult decisions. Yet she confessed that she hated decision-making. In *Waiting on God* she wrote, 'The most beautiful life possible has always seemed to me to be one where everything is determined, either by the pressure of circumstances or by impulses ... and where there is never any room for choice.'

Many people would echo that, which helps to explain the huge amount of newsprint devoted to star signs and horoscopes. Human beings long to peer into the future. Alas, God seldom allows this. But some Christians think they have the ultimate get-out as far as decision-making is concerned: put the responsibility onto God! For he is the Good Shepherd – and shepherds guide their sheep.

'Hunt the plan'

Some Christians talk about God's blueprint for their lives. They believe that God has a plan for them mapped out in advance, and they ask him to make this clear to them. There is some value in this approach, but I have serious reservations about the way it is sometimes applied. For it can shift our attention from the right question (how can I do God's will?) into a guessing game called 'hunt the plan'.

I know a Christian who lived in torment for several years, because he believed in the Blueprint God. He felt he had made a bad decision and taken a false turning a few years earlier. As a result he was convinced that the rest of his life was doomed to be lived according to a second-rate emergency plan. In my view this is a false and tragic view of God's interaction with us.

> To do the right thing is often the right thing to do.
>
> *Alec Douglas-Home*

11

For one thing, there is no such thing as a doctrine of Christian infallibility. True, we have the Scriptures to direct us, God's Son to inspire us, and the Holy Spirit to guide us. The fact remains that 'we all make many mistakes' as St James put it (James 3.2 RSV).

God's relationship with us is dynamic, not static, and a piece of music helped me to grasp this. On the radio I heard a composition by Terry Riley called *In C*. The composer did not give hard and fast rules to be followed by the players. Instead, he gave broad principles and key ideas, and asked the musicians to co-operate in the composition of the music, which was different each time it was played. In contrast, Béla Bartók wrote his string quartets with a whole set of detailed instructions to the instrumentalists, in an attempt to get the notes, the pace and the mood exactly as he wanted them.

In his relationship with us, God is much more like Riley than Bartók. He gives us guidelines – and a lot of space. Imagine that I have made what I now regard as a bad decision. Does this mean that I have lost my way, or strayed from 'the plan'? Perhaps. If so, does this mean that I must settle for second-best for evermore? No!

A key Bible verse is Romans 8.28, '... we know that in all things God works for the good of those who love him.' Note: *'in all things'*.

We worship the God of new beginnings. In our imagination we can hear God say: 'It doesn't matter *where* you happen to be in life's maze, for I am greater than your circumstances. If you want to make the most of your life then offer it to me, and from that moment on we'll make the best of it together. Take heart, for I shall prepare endless good ways for you to walk in.'

In one sense, God has a fresh 'plan' for our lives every morning. This depends on where we've got to in the maze of life. Each day carries new possibilities and is always brimful of redemption, no matter how great the mess and muddle we've made of life thus far.

God never gives up on us, any more than he gave up on Peter after his denial of Jesus. He does not offer us a blueprint. Instead, God offers us *himself*. And he has no second-best.

I was told of a collective which designs and weaves handmade carpets. If a member makes a mistake, they

YORK COURSES

Where is God...?

Participants:
- **Dr David Hope** (Introduction)
- **Archbishop Rowan Williams**
- **Patricia Routledge** CBE
- **Joel Edwards**
- **Dr Pauline Webb** (Summaries)

FIVE SESSIONS: **'Where is God...?'**
... when we seek happiness?
... when we face suffering?
... when we make decisions?
... when we contemplate death?
... when we try to make sense of life?

66 *The format works brilliantly* 99
Church Times review (2005)

BOOKLET: £3.50
(£2.25 each for 5 or more)

TAPE: £8.95
(£6.95 each for 5 or more)

CD: £10.95
(£8.95 each for 5 or more)

TRANSCRIPT: £5.00

ALL OF OUR PRICES INCLUDE PACKING AND SECOND CLASS POSTAGE

BETTER TOGETHER?

with
Abbot of Ampleforth
John Bell
Nicky Gumbel
Jane Williams

Introduced by
Dr David Hope

BOOKLET: £3.50
(£2.25 each for 5 or more)

TAPE: £8.95
(£6.95 each for 5 or more)

CD: £10.95
(£8.95 each for 5 or more)

TRANSCRIPT: £5.00

FIVE SESSIONS: *Family Relationships;*
Church Relationships; Relating to Strangers;
Broken Relationships;
Our Relationship with God

TOUGH TALK
Hard Sayings of Jesus

with
Bishop Tom Wright
Steve Chalke
Fr Gerard Hughes SJ
Prof Frances Young

Introduced by
Dr David Hope

BOOKLET: £2.95
(£1.95 each for 5 or more)

TAPE: £8.95
(£6.95 each for 5 or more)

CD: £10.95
(£8.95 each for 5 or more)

TRANSCRIPT: £5.00

FIVE SESSIONS: *Shrinking and Growing;*
Giving and Using; Praying and Forgiving;
Loving and Telling; Trusting and Entering

66 *I think that these courses are some of the best things that the*
Church of England has produced over the years 99 Dr David Hope

NEW WORLD, OLD FAITH

with
**Archbishop
   Rowan Williams
David Coffey
Joel Edwards
Revd Dr John
   Polkinghorne** KBE FRS
Dr Pauline Webb

Introduced by **Dr David Hope**

BOOKLET: **£2.95**
                (£1.95 each for 5 or more)

TAPE: **£8.95**
                (£6.95 each for 5 or more)

TRANSCRIPT: £5.00

FIVE SESSIONS: *Brave New World?; Environment and Ethics; Church and Family in Crisis?; One World – Many Faiths; Spirituality and Superstition*

IN THE WILDERNESS

with
**Cardinal Cormac
   Murphy-O'Connor
Archbishop
   David Hope
Revd Dr Rob Frost
Roy Jenkins
Dr Elaine Storkey**

BOOKLET: **£2.95**
                (£1.95 each for 5 or more)

TAPE: **£8.75**
                (£6.75 each for 5 or more)

TRANSCRIPT: £5.00

FIVE SESSIONS: *Jesus, Satan and the Angels; The Wilderness Today; The Church in the Wilderness; Prayer, Meditation and Scripture; Solitude, Friendship and Fellowship*

FAITH IN THE FIRE

with
**Archbishop
   David Hope
Rabbi Lionel Blue
Steve Chalke
Revd Dr Leslie
   Griffiths
Ann Widdecombe** MP

BOOKLET: **£2.75**
                (£1.75 each for 5 or more)

TAPE: **£8.50**
                (£6.50 each for 5 or more)

TRANSCRIPT: £5.00

FIVE SESSIONS: *Faith facing Facts; Faith facing Doubt; Faith facing Disaster; Faith fuelling Prayer; Faith fuelling Action*

JESUS REDISCOVERED

with
Paul Boateng MP
**Dr Lavinia Byrne
Joel Edwards
Bishop Tom Wright
Archbishop
   David Hope**

BOOKLET: **£2.75**
                (£1.75 each for 5 or more)

TAPE: **£8.50**
                (£6.50 each for 5 or more)

TRANSCRIPT: £5.00

FIVE SESSIONS: *Jesus' Life and Teaching; Following Jesus; Jesus: Saviour of the World; Jesus is Lord; Jesus and the Church*

Ideally, each group member should have their own booklet. To help make this possible, we reduce the price per booklet when you buy 5 or more.

ATTENDING, EXPLORING, ENGAGING *with*

Archbishop David Hope;
Steve Chalke; Fr Gerard Hughes SJ;
Professor Frances Young

TAPE: £7.50
(£6.50 each for 5 or more)

PHOTOCOPYABLE NOTES: £2.00

FIVE SESSIONS: *Attending to God; Attending to One Another; Exploring Our Faith; Engaging with the World in Service; Engaging with the World in Evangelism*

GREAT EVENTS, DEEP MEANINGS *with*

Revd Dr John Polkinghorne KBE FRS;
Gordon Wilson;
David Konstant - RC Bishop of Leeds;
Fiona Castle; Dame Cicely Saunders;
Archbishop David Hope

TAPE: £7.00
(£6.00 each for 5 or more)

PHOTOCOPYABLE NOTES: £2.00

SIX SESSIONS: *Christmas; Ash Wednesday; Palm Sunday; Good Friday; Easter; Pentecost*

THE TEACHING OF JESUS *with*

Steve Chalke; Professor James Dunn;
Dr Pauline Webb; Archbishop David Hope

TAPE: £7.00
(£6.00 each for 5 or more)

PHOTOCOPYABLE NOTES: £2.00

FIVE SESSIONS: *Forgiveness; God; Money; Heaven and Hell; On Being Human*

LIVE YOUR FAITH *with*

Revd Dr Donald English; Lord Tonypandy;
Fiona & Roy Castle

TAPE: £7.00
BOOKLET: £2.75
(£1.75 each for 5 or more)

SIX SESSIONS: *Jesus; Prayer; the Church; the Holy Spirit; the Bible; Service and Witness*

Also – TOPIC TAPES for individual listening

STRUGGLING/ COPING

TAPE 1: £5.00
*Living with **depression**
Living with **panic attacks***

TAPE 2: £5.00
*Living with **cancer**
Living with **bereavement***

Four in-depth conversations

SCIENCE AND CHRISTIAN FAITH
£5.00

An in-depth discussion with the **Revd Dr John Polkinghorne** KBE FRS, former Professor of Mathematical Physics at Cambridge University

EVANGELISM TODAY £5.00

with contributions by **Canon Robin Gamble**, the **Revd Brian Hoare, Bishop Gavin Reid** and **Canon Robert Warren**

FINDING FAITH £1.20
(95p each for 10 or more)

is a twenty-minute audio tape, designed for enquirers and church members. Four brief stories by people, including **Archbishop David Hope**, who have found faith.

Inexpensive! Designed as a 'give away'

PRAYER £3.50
(£2.50 each for 5 or more)

SIDE 1:
Archbishop David Hope on *Prayer*

SIDE 2:
Four Christians on praying … for healing; in danger; in tongues; with perseverance

This tape accompanies the booklet *The Archbishop's School of Prayer (see details overleaf)*

NO HIDDEN EXTRAS!
All our prices include packing and second class postage

do not unpick it. They respond to this by sitting down together and discussing how the design can be adapted to accommodate the new factor. Sometimes the result is *better* than the original design. This gives us an insight into the creative manner in which God works in our lives.

Desperate Decisions

At the 2005 G8 summit, British nurse Clare Bertschinger was interviewed about Band Aid. Back in 1984 it was Claire who inspired Bob Geldof to get it started. She was working in Ethiopia during the famine. At the feeding centre there were over 1,000 starving people, but food for only around 300 children.

She was even more horrified to discover that *she* must decide who should – and who should not – receive food. Claire said, 'When I chose a child, I put a black pen mark on their arm. The reaction of those I didn't select was incredible. I'd have expected a riot and there was simply no reaction. You could feel their hopelessness. I felt like a Nazi sentencing people to their death.'

BBC's Michael Buerk asked Claire how it felt deciding which children to select. She replied, 'It breaks my heart. What do you expect?'

An example of God's guidance

Albert Schweitzer was one of the great figures of the twentieth century. He was a leading authority on Bach, an organist of great distinction and a radical theologian with an international reputation. One day he read a magazine from the Paris Missionary Society which spoke of the need for missionaries in the Congo. The article ended like this: 'Men and women who can reply simply to the Master's call by saying, "Lord, I am coming" – those are the people whom the Church needs.'

As he closed the magazine he realised that this was God's call to him personally. So he enrolled as a medical student, and embarked on his life's major work as a doctor in Equatorial Africa. His decision was controversial, and some saw it as a waste of his unique intellectual powers. It can be understood in the light of this moving paragraph from his most famous work of theology (see Box in margin).

QUESTIONS FOR GROUPS

SUGGESTED BIBLE READING:
Luke 12.22-34

1. Raise any points from this booklet or the audio tape/CD with which you strongly agree or disagree.

2. What is the most difficult decision you ever made? Did you follow your head or your 'gut instinct'? Did it work out well – or disastrously!?

3. (a) Do you believe in the guidance of God? If so, how does he guide? Do you believe he is concerned with your small day-to-day decisions or just the really big ones?

   (b) Do you believe that God has one master plan for your life – or a new plan each day, perhaps? If the former, have you found it?

4. Which, in your view, is the better prayer for guidance and why?

   (a) Lord, please show me the way ahead.

   (b) Lord, please give me wisdom as I make this decision.

5. What do you make of the popularity of horoscopes? Should Christians ever pay attention to these?

6. A teenager asks for your views on, and prayers for, his future career. An elderly widow asks for your views and prayers for a possible move into a smaller house or retirement home. Rehearse what you might say to them both.

7. What do you make of the approach to decision-taking by Simone Weil and Albert Schweitzer? Can you empathise or were they foolish in your view? Is it sometimes right to take decisions which are contrary to 'common sense'?

8. Draw up a list of big questions facing our world which require high-level decisions e.g. designer babies, global warming.

9. (a) Some people believe that active faith always involves risk. Do you agree? Can you illustrate?

   (b) Jesus' time in the wilderness shows that decision-making can be linked with temptation. Share views on this (and experiences, if you dare!)

10. **Read Psalm 23.1** and **Proverbs 3.5-6.** How do these insights apply to our decision-making? What place do prayer, Bible reading and friendship play in decision-making?

NOTE: *You might find it helpful to read Question 6 from Session 4 to prepare for your next meeting.*

Closing meditation:
Read Joshua 24.15.

I remember good advice from a retired minister. 'If you have to choose between two paths, and you can see clearly where one of them is leading, but the other follows a course hidden from view, I would take the risky one. That will make you more dependent on God to accompany you on the way'.
(Pauline Webb)

Pray for those wrestling with difficult personal decisions and for politicians who make decisions which affect us all.

14

... when we CONTEMPLATE DEATH?

Like millions of other people, before going to bed I clean my teeth. One evening it struck me that I will not perform this simple, routine task for ever. I will clean my teeth on a finite, though unknown, number of occasions.

This is hardly a profound insight but it did hit me with some force. It was one more prompt to make me consider my mortality. Such nudges come in various forms:

- A friend or relative falls seriously ill.
- The phone rings and news of a sudden death is announced (that has happened to me twice in the last ten days).
- A birthday with a nought at the end ('Gosh, not another one already'). I recall that my younger sister wept bitterly on her twentieth birthday because 'life is now behind me'!
- A walk in an ancient city. I sometimes walk in York and think of the feet which trod those same pavements one hundred years ago. Not a single walker from that generation is alive today.

Mercifully – and properly – most of us are too busy most of the time to allow such deep Hamlet-type questions to preoccupy us. The cat needs feeding or the dog needs walking (or both!). We must get to work or take our children to school. We plan our holidays and go out for a meal with friends. We prune the roses and phone the plumber.

All these activities are necessary and wholesome. But it is equally necessary and wholesome to pause just occasionally, to consider the inescapable fact that each and every one of us is a mortal human being.

Philip of Macedon, father of Alexander the Great, instructed a slave to come to him every day and declare, 'Remember, Philip, one day you will die'. Some modern philosophers – most famously the German existentialist Martin Heidegger – tell us that we are not living an authentic life unless we take this central fact into account.

Here and now

Philip of Macedon was a practical man. He wanted that daily reminder of his mortality to influence the way he lived. It helped him to order his priorities and get a true perspective on his activities.

> Sometimes confronting the fact of one's death is amazingly vivifying. But I don't want to pose as somebody who has solved this problem – I share it.
>
> *Richard Chartres,*
> *Bishop of London*

Taking death into account can take many forms, of course.

- *The way of hedonism* 'Eat, drink and be merry, for tomorrow we die' (Isaiah 22.13; 1 Corinthians 15.32). This famous saying from the Bible spells out one classic response. Life is short, so cram it with pleasure. It is easy to sneer at this superficial approach, but many who seek to follow Christ find that hedonism is the main rival to discipleship. I certainly do. The notion of a comfortable, undemanding life, filled with activities, objects, and people who give me pleasure, is very attractive indeed. These things have their place, of course. But I, at least, need a stern reminder that I follow the One who said, 'I came not to be served, but to serve' (Mark 10.45).

- *The way of stoicism* Although stoicism goes back to the ancient Greek world, this approach is most easily characterised by the British 'stiff upper lip'. *Duty* is a key word. Stoicism tries to take life's knocks on the chin. We can do nothing to stop death – the biggest knock of all – so best not to think too much about it.

- *The way of Christ* The Christian approach is markedly different from either of the above, although it does include some elements from both. Jesus himself was accused of being 'a glutton and a drunkard' (Matthew 11.19). He liked parties! On the other hand, the notion of *perseverance* in the face of adversity and suffering is a recurrent theme in the New Testament (e.g. Hebrews 12.1-3).

The way of Christ is not mere hedonism, nor undiluted stoicism. A phrase from a modern Eucharistic Prayer gets the balance perfectly when it talks about 'our duty and our joy'. Yes, there are lots of 'oughts' in discipleship. We are under an inescapable obligation to love and to serve one another. But the Christian life is – or should be – shot through with joy. The Christian way brings a new quality of life, arising from the indwelling Spirit of Jesus. The Christ within us is the One who assures us that, 'I have come to bring life in all its abundance' (John 10.10).

Pie in the sky?

A whole session on death. If people outside the church – especially young people – heard that groups all over the country were discussing death, they might be dismissive. This might confirm their belief that Christianity is a faith for older people seeking 'pie in the sky when you die'. Others might accuse us of being morbid and preoccupied with death.

It is true that the cross of Christ has become *the* symbol of the Christian faith. Rightly so, for the New Testament places great emphasis on that awesome event. It is for good reason that we call the terrible day on which Jesus died, *Good* Friday. We do so, not because we are fixated on death but because we celebrate *life*. Just how the death of Jesus sets us free is a mystery. But it is a mystery which brings life, light and hope to millions in the modern world.

By his death and resurrection, Jesus defeated sin and death. St Paul rejoices that 'Death has been swallowed up in victory'. As the great John Donne, Dean of St Paul's Cathedral from 1621 to 1631, wrote:

'One short sleep past, we wake eternally,
And death shall be no more; death, thou shalt die'.

The vibrant life of heaven

When it talks of the glories of heaven, the Bible does so in terms of physical resurrection, rather than spiritual survival. By *resurrection* the New Testament writers do not mean mere *resuscitation*. What is raised will be far more glorious than what is 'sown' – just as the butterfly is more beautiful and vibrant than the caterpillar.

In this area, modern Christians are sometimes rather tentative about embracing the full-blooded faith of the New Testament. Perhaps near-death experiences should encourage us to be bolder. The jury is still out about their true significance – serious research on them is being conducted in some of our universities. It may well be that a physiological explanation will emerge. That will not matter in the least as far as the Christian hope is concerned.

At this point I want to focus on the undeniable fact that people who 'come back from the brink' often speak of light and warmth, a sense of being welcomed, and a feeling of supreme well-being. This accurately reflects New Testament teaching about heaven.

The Bible does not pretend to probe too deeply into the mystery of life beyond the grave. But it does promise transformation and glory. Life on earth is the shadow; life in heaven will be full of substance. You will still be recognisably 'you'. You will not simply add your little drop of energy to the great cosmic consciousness, but will be fully alive in a way that you can only dream of now.

The book of Revelation assures us that there will be no more tears and no more pain. Heaven will be a place of joy and love and light. St John catches this New Testament mixture of mystery and knowledge like this: 'Dear friends, now we are children of God, and what we will be has not yet been made known. But we know that when Christ appears, we shall be like him, for we shall see him as he is' (1 John 3.2).

*

Where is God when we contemplate death? He is there beside us, reminding us that his Son also walked through 'the valley of the shadow of death' – and emerged into glorious sunlight. He has gone before us, in order to prepare a place for us. As the old translation puts it, 'in my Father's house are many mansions' (John 14.2).

> When I approach the pearly gates, I'd like to hear a champagne cork popping, an orchestra tuning up, and the sound of my mother laughing.
>
> *Patricia Routledge*

The cross at St Mary's Roman Catholic church in Matara, Sri Lanka, which was almost completely destroyed by the 2004 Boxing Day Tsunami. (With kind permission of the Ceylon Bible Society).

QUESTIONS FOR GROUPS

SUGGESTED BIBLE READING:
Philippians 1.19-26

1. Raise any points from this booklet or the audio tape/CD with which you strongly agree or disagree.

2. Are you afraid of
   (a) dying?
   (b) being dead – no longer existing in this world?

3. Many modern people would prefer a sudden death. Previous generations tended to favour a process of dying which afforded time to prepare for 'a good death'. What do you hope for?

4. It is said that Pope John Paul II gave the world an example of 'a good death'. What can we learn from him about living and dying?

5. (a) Do you believe in heaven? Do you believe you will go there? If so, why?
   (b) Do you believe in hell? If so, who will go there and what will it be like?

6. Have you made any preparations for your death e.g. a will or advance directive ('Living Will')? What ingredients do you want in your funeral service and what sort of mood should it have e.g. solemn, joyful?

7. What do you make of the comments of the teacher at Fettes College? (Box on page 16).
   How does accepting and facing our mortality affect our day-to-day lives?

8. In your view is there enough of Good Friday in the week-by-week worship of your church? Is there enough Easter joy? Could the balance be improved – if so, how?

9. Someone of another faith asks how the events of Good Friday and Easter Sunday relate to you personally. What would you say?

10. **Read Revelation 21.1-4.** That same enquirer asks how you envisage the life of heaven. Answers please – though not on a postcard! (You may find it helpful to re-read the last 6 paragraphs of this chapter.)

Closing meditation:

Read John 11.25.

When Cardinal Hume was diagnosed with terminal cancer he rang to tell Timothy Wright, the Abbot of Ampleforth. The abbot said: "Congratulations! That's brilliant news. I wish I was coming with you." The Cardinal replied, "Thank you, Timothy. Everyone else has burst into tears."

Pray for your local hospice and anyone known to you to be terminally ill or struggling with bereavement.

Louis Armstrong sings:
　I see trees of green,
　　Red roses too ...
　And I think to myself,
　'What a wonderful world'.